How To Start Business In Ultimate Way

A Steps Roadmap to Business Triumph

Naomi Jaurez

Table of contents

Chapter I:Green Supply Chain Management

Green Supply Chain Management:
Implementing eco-friendly practices across the supply chain is vital for firms aiming to decrease their environmental impact and satisfy sustainability objectives. Here's a step-by-step tutorial on how firms might do this:

1. Sustainable Sourcing of Raw Materials:Identify sustainable suppliers for raw materials that stress ecologically responsible operations.
   - Consider certifications like Fair Trade, Organic, or Forest Stewardship Council (FSC) for ethical and sustainable sourcing.

2. Efficient Production Processes:Implement lean manufacturing techniques to decrease waste and energy usage.

- Invest in energy-efficient equipment and technology to decrease resource use.

3. Packaging and Product Design: Optimize product packaging to reduce resources and waste.
  - Design items with durability and recyclability in mind, using eco-friendly materials.

4.Transportation and Logistics: Opt for energy-efficient transportation choices, such as hybrid or electric automobiles.
  - Consolidate shipments to decrease transportation emissions and expenses.
  - Explore alternate transportation options like train or sea to decrease carbon impact.

5. Inventory Management:Implement just-in-time inventory methods to decrease excess stock and related waste.
  - Use inventory management tools to monitor and regulate stock levels effectively.

6. Supplier Collaboration: Work closely with suppliers to encourage sustainable practices within their operations.

- Encourage suppliers to use ecologically friendly packaging and delivery techniques.

7.Recycling and trash Reduction: Establish recycling initiatives throughout the supply chain to decrease trash going to landfills.

- Reuse and recycle resources whenever feasible, such as pallets or packing materials.

8.Energy Efficiency:Implement energy-efficient technology and procedures inside warehouses and distribution facilities.

- Consider on-site renewable energy sources like solar panels to power buildings.

9.Measurement and Reporting:Track important sustainability parameters, such as carbon emissions, trash creation, and energy consumption.

- Report on progress and share sustainability accomplishments with stakeholders.

10.Continuous Improvement:Regularly analyze the supply chain for opportunities of improvement.

- Engage workers and suppliers in sustainability projects and seek their advice on upgrades.

11.Compliance and rules:Stay knowledgeable about environmental rules and maintain compliance across the supply chain.

- Be proactive in implementing industry-specific sustainability standards and certifications.

12.Consumer Education and Engagement: Communicate your commitment to eco-friendly practices to customers.

- Encourage customers to make sustainable choices by giving information on product labels and via marketing initiatives

Chapter II:Renewable Energy Adoption

Renewable Energy Adoption: Transitioning to renewable energy sources like solar and wind power presents numerous advantages and obstacles for organizations looking to decrease their carbon footprint:

*Benefits:
1.Environmental Impact Reduction:Switching to renewable energy greatly decreases a company's carbon impact. Solar and wind power create energy with minimal to no greenhouse gas emissions, helping battle climate change.

2.Cost Savings: Over time, renewable energy may lead to huge cost reductions. While the initial investment in solar panels or wind turbines may be significant, the continuous running expenses are frequently cheaper compared to fossil fuels.

3.Energy Independence:Renewable energy sources give a degree of energy independence. Companies may produce own power, minimizing dependency on variable fossil fuel costs and possible supply interruptions.

4.Constant Energy prices:Renewable energy sources offer constant and predictable prices since they depend on free and plentiful resources (sunlight and wind). This steadiness helps safeguard enterprises from energy price volatility.

5.Positive Brand Image:Adopting renewable energy displays a commitment to sustainability and environmental responsibility. It may strengthen a company's image and attract environmentally concerned consumers and investment.

6.Incentives and Tax Credits:Many governments give incentives, tax credits, and subsidies to firms that engage in renewable energy, making the switch financially advantageous.

*Challenges:
1. High Initial Costs:The installation of solar panels or wind turbines might involve a considerable upfront expenditure, which may be a barrier for certain companies, especially smaller ones.

2. Intermittency: Solar and wind power production may be intermittent and depending on weather conditions. Businesses may require backup power sources or energy storage technologies to assure a steady energy supply.

3.Room Requirements:Solar panels and wind turbines need room for installation. This might be an issue for firms with limited accessible land or rooftop space.

4.Integration and Compatibility:Transitioning to renewable energy may involve changes to existing infrastructure and electrical systems to guarantee compatibility and efficient energy distribution.

5.Regulatory and Permitting Hurdles:Navigating the regulatory framework for renewable energy projects may be difficult and time-consuming, possibly delaying implementation.

6.Technological Advancements: As renewable energy technology improves, organizations may need to spend in modernizing their systems to remain competitive and efficient.

7.Resource Availability:The practicality of solar and wind power relies on geographical location. Businesses in places with low sunshine or wind may confront difficulty in utilizing these resources successfully.

8.Maintenance and Durability:Renewable energy systems need frequent maintenance to guarantee optimum performance. Businesses must budget for continuous repair and possible equipment replacement.

ChapterIII:Corporate Social Responsibility (CSR):

Corporate Social Responsibility (CSR): Corporate Social Responsibility (CSR) plays a significant part in sustainable corporate operations, spanning philanthropy, community involvement, and ethical labor practices. Here's an evaluation of how CSR helps to sustainability in various areas:

1. Philanthropy:Community Investment:CSR includes philanthropic activities where firms donate resources, such as finances or commodities, to assist charity causes. These contributions might include gifts to charitable organizations, disaster relief operations, or financing for education and healthcare programs.

*Environmental Causes: Many firms participate in environmental philanthropy by funding activities relating to conservation, replanting, and sustainable energy. This corresponds with sustainability aims, since it contributes to a healthy earth.

*Employee Engagement:Philanthropic activities may enhance staff morale and engagement. Employees frequently like working with organizations that are socially responsible and active in philanthropic initiatives.

2Community Engagement:Stakeholder Collaboration: Engaging with local communities and stakeholders is a vital part of CSR. Businesses may cooperate with communities to solve common concerns, such as environmental preservation or economic growth, promoting a feeling of shared responsibility.

*Education and Skill Development:CSR activities frequently entail funding educational and skill development programs within communities. This not only helps people but also leads to a better trained and employable workforce.

*Positive Public Relations:Engaging with communities and tackling local concerns may increase a company's image. It indicates a commitment to being a good corporate citizen, which may lead to improved consumer loyalty and favorable brand reputation.

*3. Ethical Labor Practices:CSR stresses ethical labor practices, including fair salaries, safe working conditions, and compliance with labor regulations. Treating workers ethically is not just a moral responsibility but also adds to a sustainable and engaged staff.

*Diversity and Inclusion:Promoting diversity and inclusion inside the workplace is a vital element of CSR. Embracing diversity leads to a more imaginative and adaptive staff and develops a culture of equality.

Supply Chain Responsibility:CSR goes beyond a company's direct staff to its supplier chain. Ensuring that suppliers adhere to ethical labor standards is vital for sustainability and avoiding reputational issues.

Chapter IV:Waste Reduction and Recycling Initiatives

Waste Reduction and Recycling Initiatives:
Minimizing trash output and boosting recycling activities within a corporation are essential steps toward sustainability and lowering environmental impact. Here are techniques to attain these goals:

1. Waste Reduction Strategies:

a.Source Reduction: Reduce waste at the source by utilizing fewer resources in manufacturing and packing. Choose providers that reduce superfluous packing.

b.Product Design:Design items to be more durable, repairable, and recyclable. Consider cradle-to-cradle design concepts.

c.Inventory Management:Implement just-in-time inventory techniques to eliminate surplus goods that may become waste.

d.Lean Manufacturing: Adopt lean concepts to decrease waste in manufacturing operations, such as decreasing defects and excess inventories.

2. Recycling Strategies:

a.Comprehensive Recycling Programs:Establish recycling programs for multiple waste streams, including paper, plastics, glass, electronics, and hazardous items.

b.Employee Education:Train personnel to properly sort and dispose of recyclables and provide clear labeling for recycling bins.

c.Waste Audits: Conduct frequent waste audits to identify potential for enhanced recycling and trash reduction.

d.Recycling Partnerships:Collaborate with recycling firms and waste management services to enable effective recycling and disposal of items.

3. Sustainable Packaging:

a. Eco-Friendly Materials: Use recyclable, biodegradable, or compostable packaging materials wherever feasible.

b. Minimalist package:Adopt minimalist package designs that decrease resources while keeping product integrity.

c.Take-Back Programs: Establish take-back programs for packaging or items to guarantee appropriate recycling or disposal.

4. Waste-to-Energy and Upcycling:

a. Explore Waste-to-Energy: Consider turning specific waste streams into energy using processes like anaerobic digestion or incineration with energy recovery.

b. Upcycling Initiatives: Explore possibilities to upcycle waste materials into new goods or components.

5. Supplier Engagement:

a.Supplier Sustainability:Encourage suppliers to embrace sustainable and eco-friendly packaging and materials.

b. Closed-Loop Supply Chain:Explore closed-loop supply chain models where providers take back and recycle resources.

6. Circular Economy Practices:

a. Embrace Circular concepts: Implement circular economy concepts where items and materials are reused, reconditioned, or recycled to prolong their lives.

b.Product Stewardship: Take responsibility for the environmental effect of your goods throughout their full lifetime, including disposal.

7. Monitoring and Reporting:

a.Data Collection:Monitor trash creation and recycling rates to measure progress.

b.Transparency:Share waste reduction and recycling efforts with stakeholders through sustainability reports.

8. Employee Involvement:

   a.Engage staff:Involve staff in sustainability activities to create ideas and promote a culture of waste reduction and recycling.

Chapter V:Circular Economy Approaches

Circular Economy Approaches: The notion of a circular economy offers a paradigm change from the old linear "take-make-dispose" model of production and consumption to a more sustainable and regenerative approach. In a circular economy, items and materials are reused, refurbished, or recycled, thereby decreasing waste and boosting resource efficiency. Here's an examination of this topic and how firms might embrace it:

Key Principles of a Circular Economy:
1.Design for Longevity:Products are built to have longer lifespans, be readily repairable, and utilize materials that can be recycled or reused.

2.Reuse and Refurbishment:Instead of abandoning things, they are restored and resold, prolonging their useful life.

3.Recycling and Resource Recovery:Materials from items at the end of their life are recycled into new products or materials.

4.Product-as-a-Service:Companies change from selling items to delivering them as services, promoting responsible use and ownership.

5.Trash Elimination: The objective is to limit trash output, with any waste created being considered a potential resource.

*Benefits of a Circular Economy:

- Resource Conservation: Maximizes the utilization of current resources, lowering the demand for additional raw materials and lessening resource scarcity.

- Trash Reduction:Drastically minimizes trash creation and landfill disposal, minimizing the environmental effect.

- Energy Efficiency: Recycling and refurbishing often consume less energy than creating new goods from raw materials.

-Cost Savings:Can lead to cost savings via lower material and waste disposal expenditures and better resource efficiency.

-Environmental Benefits:Reduces greenhouse gas emissions, pollution, and strain on ecosystems.

How Businesses Can Embrace a Circular Economy Model:

1.Rethink Product Design:Design items for durability, modularity, and simplicity of disassembly to promote repair and reuse.

- Use eco-friendly and recyclable materials in product manufacture.

2.Product-as-a-Service (PaaS):Shift from selling goods to delivering them as services (e.g., leasing or subscription models).

- Maintain ownership and responsibility for product maintenance, repair, and end-of-life management.

3. Remanufacturing and Refurbishment:Develop techniques for refurbishing and remanufacturing items to prolong their lifetime.
   - Create incentives for consumers to return items for refurbishing.

4.Reverse Logistics: Establish efficient processes for gathering, classifying, and transferring spent items and materials.

5.Collaboration and Partnerships: Collaborate with suppliers, customers, and stakeholders to develop closed-loop supply chains.
   - Engage in collaborations with recycling and trash management organizations.

6.Consumer Education: Educate consumers about the advantages of a circular economy and how they may help by making sustainable choices.

7.Regulatory Compliance:Stay knowledgeable about and compliance with applicable environmental legislation and standards.

8.Monitoring and Reporting: Track and report on important circular economy performance metrics, such as recycling rates and resource utilization.

Chapter VI:Sustainable Product Design

Sustainable Product Design: Designing goods with sustainability in mind is a vital step in reducing environmental impact and fostering a more eco-friendly approach to production and consumption. This procedure incorporates considerations for durability, recyclability, and the usage of eco-friendly materials. Here's a deeper look at each aspect:

1. Durability:
 - Materials Selection: Choose materials recognized for their durability, endurance, and resilience to wear and strain. This may include metals, high-quality polymers, or composite materials engineered for durability.

-Quality Control:Implement strict quality control methods throughout manufacture to guarantee that items fulfill durability criteria. This involves testing for structural integrity and wear resistance.
-Modularity:Design goods with modular components that can be readily changed or updated as required, prolonging the product's total lifetime.
-Maintenance Accessibility:Make it simple for users or technicians to access and fix components or conduct regular maintenance, decreasing the chance of disposal due to minor faults.

2. Recyclability:

- Material Identification:Use standardized labeling and identification procedures to clearly identify the materials used in the product. This streamlines recycling operations.

-Material Compatibility: Ensure that various components of the product are manufactured from materials that can be separated and recycled easily.

-Design for Disassembly: Design items with ease of disassembly in mind, enabling for effective separation of recyclable elements from non-recyclable ones.

 -Recycling Partnerships:Collaborate with recycling facilities or programs to provide channels for recycling the product at the end of its life.

 - Consumer Education:Educate consumers on how to properly dispose of or recycle the product, including information on local recycling facilities and procedures.

3. Eco-Friendly Materials:

 -Sustainable Sourcing:Choose materials from sustainable sources, such as certified wood or recycled metals, to limit the environmental effect of material extraction.

 - Biodegradable Materials: Consider employing biodegradable or compostable materials for components that don't need long-term durability.

-Low-Impact Manufacturing:Opt for materials that demand reduced energy and water inputs during manufacture and have minimum chemical emissions.

- Non-Toxic Materials:Prioritize materials that are non-toxic and safe for both humans and the environment.

-Life Cycle Assessment:Conduct a life cycle assessment (LCA) to analyze the environmental effect of materials and make educated decisions.

- Innovative Alternatives:Explore novel materials like recycled plastics, bamboo, or mycelium-based materials that are eco-friendly and suited for many product uses.

Chapter VII: Environmental effect analyses

Environmental effect analyses: Businesses may undertake extensive analyses of their environmental effect and establish strategies for improvement using an organized and methodical process. Here's a step-by-step instruction on how to achieve this:

1. Define Objectives and Scope:
   - Clearly identify the aims and objectives of the environmental assessment. Determine the scope of the evaluation, including the precise components of the company activities to be reviewed.

2. Gather Data:
   - Collect data on numerous environmental issues, such as energy use, water usage, trash creation, emissions, and resource utilization. Ensure data correctness and consistency.

3. Identify Environmental Aspects:

 - Identify the key environmental components and implications of your company activity. Consider concerns like air and water pollution, habitat change, and resource depletion.

4. Conduct a Life Cycle Assessment (LCA):

 - Use a life cycle assessment to examine the environmental effect of your goods or services across their full life cycle, from raw material extraction through disposal.

5. Set Baseline Performance Metrics:

 - Establish baseline performance indicators for each selected environmental element. These measurements will serve as a reference point for assessing progress.

6. Regulatory Compliance:

- Ensure compliance with environmental laws and regulations relevant to your sector and area.

7. Analyze Data:

- Analyze the acquired data to find trends, patterns, and areas of concern. Consider completing a SWOT analysis to identify strengths, weaknesses, opportunities, and threats connected to environmental impact.

8. Stakeholder Engagement:

- Engage with stakeholders, including workers, customers, suppliers, and the local community, to obtain thoughts and concerns relating to environmental impact.

9. Develop Improvement Plans:

- Based on the data analysis and stakeholder engagement, build specific improvement strategies for addressing identified environmental concerns.

10. Prioritize Actions:

- Prioritize measures based on the severity of environmental effect, practicality, and opportunity for improvement.

11. Resource Allocation:

- Allocate resources, including finance, manpower, and technology, to assist the execution of improvement programs.

12. Implement Changes:

- Implement the specified activities and strategies to decrease environmental impact. Monitor progress and alter methods as required.

13. Performance Tracking:

- Continuously monitor and measure environmental performance using the set metrics. Compare performance versus baseline data and objectives.

14. Reporting and Transparency:

- Communicate your environmental efforts and progress to stakeholders via frequent reporting and transparency initiatives.

15. Continuous Improvement:

- Embrace a culture of continuous improvement by routinely assessing and revising environmental improvement plans and initiatives.

16. Certification and Recognition:

- Consider seeking environmental certifications or awards that validate your sustainability efforts and demonstrate your commitment to stakeholders.

17. Training and Education:

- Provide training and instruction to workers to ensure they understand their duties in reducing the company's environmental effect.

18. Collaboration:

- Collaborate with industry peers, governmental agencies, and environmental groups to exchange best practices and get insights into creative solutions.

ChapterVIII:Employee Engagement in Sustainability

Employee Engagement in Sustainability: Employees play a significant role in pushing sustainability efforts inside a firm. Their participation and dedication to sustainable practices may greatly benefit the company's environmental and social responsibility initiatives. Here's an outline of the role of workers and techniques for developing a culture of sustainability:

Role of Employees in Driving Sustainability:

1.Innovation and Idea Generation:Employees frequently bring significant insights and recommendations for enhancing sustainability. Encourage them to contribute recommendations for decreasing waste, preserving resources, or adopting eco-friendly behaviors.

2.Daily Practices:Employees directly impact day-to-day operations. Their decisions regarding energy consumption, waste reduction, and resource conservation may cumulatively contribute to major environmental effect.

3. Advocacy and Outreach: Engaged workers may become champions for sustainability both inside and beyond the firm. They may promote awareness, encourage others, and add to the company's excellent reputation.

4. Compliance and Reporting:Employees are accountable for following to sustainability rules and procedures. Their attention in following rules guarantees that the firm fulfills its sustainability objectives.

Strategies for Fostering a Culture of Sustainability:

1. Leadership Commitment: Top-level executives and leaders should clearly support sustainability projects and set an example for others to follow.

2. Clear Sustainability Goals: Establish clear and quantifiable sustainability objectives that correspond with the organization's values and purpose. Communicate these aims to all staff.

3. Education and Training: Provide training and education on sustainable techniques and their relevance. Make sure staff understand how their responsibilities contribute to sustainability goals.

4. Engagement and Participation: Encourage workers to actively engage in sustainability initiatives, committees, or projects. Involve them in decision-making processes linked to sustainability.

5. Recognition and Rewards: Recognize and recognize personnel for their contributions to sustainability initiatives. Consider incentives, rewards, or recognition programs to inspire involvement.

6.Communication:Maintain open and honest communication regarding sustainability objectives and progress. Share success stories and highlight the good effect of employee participation.

7.Feedback Mechanisms:Create avenues for workers to express comments, recommendations, and concerns relating to sustainability. Act on their suggestions to enhance sustainable practices.

8.Integration into Job Roles:Integrate sustainability duties into job descriptions and performance assessments. Make sustainability a part of everyone's employment.

9.Resource Allocation: Allocate resources and funds to support sustainability activities. Ensure that teams have the appropriate tools and resources to execute sustainable practices.

10.Cross-Functional cooperation: Promote cooperation across diverse departments and teams to create and execute sustainable solutions that cut beyond organizational boundaries.

11.Measurement and Reporting:Continuously monitor and report on sustainable performance. Share success updates with staff to keep them informed and motivated.

12. Celebrating Milestones:Celebrate sustainability milestones and successes with staff to generate a feeling of pride and ownership in sustainability projects.

13.Continuous Improvement:Encourage a culture of continuous improvement by frequently examining and upgrading sustainability initiatives based on emerging best practices and new technology.

Chapter IX:Sustainable Marketing and Consumer Awareness

Sustainable Marketing and Consumer Awareness: Effective communication of sustainability activities to consumers is vital for organizations aiming to engage and educate their customers on their environmental and social responsibility initiatives. It also underscores the necessity of conscientious consumer decisions. Here's an examination of these aspects:

1. Communicating Sustainability Efforts:

a. Transparency:Be open about your sustainability activities. Share information about your objectives, successes, and obstacles. Transparency develops confidence with customers.

b.Clear Messaging:Use clear and succinct language to describe your sustainability efforts. Avoid jargon and technical phrases that can mislead customers.

c. Storytelling: Tell interesting tales about your sustainable journey. Highlight milestones, accomplishments, and the beneficial effect of your activities.

d.Visuals: Use visuals, such as infographics, movies, and photos, to present information about your sustainability initiatives in an entertaining and easy-to-understand manner.

e.Labels and Certifications:Display applicable sustainability certifications or labels on goods and packaging to demonstrate your commitment to ecologically and socially responsible activities.

f.Sustainability Reports:Publish yearly or quarterly sustainability reports that outline your initiatives, accomplishments, and future objectives. Make these reports available to customers.

g. Online Presence:Use your website and social media channels to give in-depth information on sustainability activities. Engage with customers via various platforms to answer queries and gain feedback.

2. Importance of Conscious Consumer Choices:

a. Supporting Ethical Practices:When customers make conscious decisions, they support firms that value ethical and environmental operations. This generates a market demand for responsible goods and services.

b. Driving Innovation: Conscious customersurge firms to innovate and developsustainable alternatives, lessening theenvironmental and social impact of goodsand services.

c. Environmental Impact: Consumers may decrease their carbon footprint by purchasing items with reduced energy use, recyclable packaging, or sustainably produced materials.

d.Promoting Accountability: Conscious customers hold corporations responsible for their behavior. Companies are more inclined to make beneficial adjustments when they know customers are paying attention.

e. Social Responsibility:Consumers who support socially responsible firms contribute to the welfare of communities and people involved in the supply chain.

f. Market Transformation: As more customers make mindful decisions, the market changes toward sustainability. This motivates other firms to adopt ethical practices to stay competitive.

3. Collaborative Initiatives:

a.Partnerships: Collaborate with like-minded organizations and advocacy groups to raise the message of sustainability and promote conscious consumerism.

b. Consumer Education: Invest in consumer education initiatives to enlighten and empower consumers to make informed decisions based on sustainable criteria.

4. Measuring Impact:

a. Feedback Loops: Establish feedback channels to get information from customers on your sustainability activities. Use this input to enhance and improve your projects.

b.Metrics and KPIs:Use key performance indicators (KPIs) to monitor the effect of your sustainability actions and communicate these findings with customers.

Chapter X:Government Regulations and Incentives

Government Regulations and Incentives: Government policies and incentives have a vital influence in influencing and promoting sustainable business practices. They may encourage enterprises to implement ecologically and socially responsible practices by granting financial incentives, creating laws, and providing a supporting regulatory framework. Here's a study of how government policies and incentives effect sustainable business practices:

1. Tax Incentives:

 - Tax Credits: Governments may grant tax credits or deductions to enterprises who invest in sustainability projects, such as energy-efficient equipment, renewable energy systems, or research and development of green technology.

- Tax Exemptions:Some governments allow tax breaks on revenue derived from eco-friendly activities, such recycling or renewable energy generation.

- Depreciation Benefits: Accelerated depreciation schedules may be used to sustainable investments, enabling organizations to recoup capital expenditures more rapidly.

- Carbon Pricing:Carbon pricing methods, such as carbon taxes or cap-and-trade systems, may promote emissions reduction by making carbon-intensive activities more costly and encouraging enterprises to adopt cleaner technology.

2. Environmental Regulations:

-Emissions Standards:Government laws frequently establish emissions requirements that firms must comply to, stimulating investment in greener technology and practices.

- Trash Management Regulations:Laws controlling trash disposal and recycling encourage companies to limit waste creation and embrace sustainable waste management methods.

- Renewable Energy Mandates: Some areas demand a portion of energy output to originate from renewable sources, driving firms to invest in clean energy solutions.

- Resource Conservation:Regulations connected to resource conservation, such as water consumption limitations or restrictions on resource exploitation, force enterprises to adopt more sustainable practices.

3. Grants and Subsidies:

- Government Grants: Businesses may get grants and subsidies to assist sustainable projects, research, or technological development, making it financially possible to invest in green efforts.

4. Environmental Certification and Standards:

-Government-Backed Certifications:Governments may develop or approve environmental certifications and standards that firms may seek, offering legitimacy and recognition for sustainability activities.

5. Research and Development Funding:

-R&D Grants:*llGovernments typically give grants or subsidies for research and development in sustainable technology and practices.

6. Market Access and Trade Agreements:

- Access to Markets:Sustainable goods and practices might obtain greater access to international markets via trade agreements that promote environmental and social responsibility.

7. Reporting and Disclosure Requirements:

- Transparency Regulations:Governments may mandate firms to report their environmental and social implications, fostering accountability and transparency.

8. Public Procurement Policies:

- **Government Purchases:** Governments may impact sustainable practices by prioritizing goods and services that satisfy particular environmental and social criteria in their procurement rules.

9. Incentive Programs for Employees:*

- **Tax-Free Commuter Benefits:** Tax advantages for businesses giving eco-friendly commuting choices, such public transport passes or bike-sharing memberships.

- Green Employee perks:Tax incentives for firms giving green perks including eco-friendly childcare services.

10. Support for Innovation:

-Research and Development (R&D) Tax Credits:** Encouraging innovation by giving tax credits for R&D expenditures focused on sustainable technologies and practices.

Government regulations and incentives play a crucial role in influencing the corporate environment and promoting the adoption of sustainable practices. They establish a favorable climate for enterprises to invest in sustainability, minimize their environmental imprint, and contribute to larger social and environmental objectives. Ultimately, this combination of government assistance and enterprise sustainability initiatives may lead to favorable economic, social, and environmental effects.